MW01172865

ENRICHING GRACE COMMENTARY OF EPHESIANS

Understanding the Faith

Jacob Harris

Enriching Grace Ministries

Copyright © 2021 Enriching Grace Ministries

All rights reserved

No part of this book may be reproduced, or stored in a retrieval system,
or transmitted in any form or by any means, electronic, mechanical,
photocopying, recording, or otherwise, without express written permission
of the publisher.

Cover design by: Canva
ISBN: 9798474047010
Imprint: Independently published
Printed in the United States of America

This commentary is dedicated my wonderful family, my loving better half, and the my Savior Jesus Christ.

CONTENTS

PREFACE

Greetings and thank you for reading this commentary. There are plenty of valuable commentaries on Ephesians with an tremendous amount of information to offer for your spiritual enriching. The question is however- Why this commentary?

This is an excellent question. I would simply reply by asking you, the reader, the same question. Why this commentary? What are you looking for as you read through Ephesians? If you discern the answer to this question for yourself, you will understand why you would read this study.

Some commentaries are excellent at "putting feet" to the original Greek that Ephesians was written in. I am not a Greek scholar. Some commentaries are great at utilizing Ephesians as a defense for their denominational beliefs. Although I may lean some ways, I do not identify with a denomination. The list goes on.

Nonetheless, I do bring a well-studied, Scriptural, plethora of practical Biblical teaching to the table. My goal is to "put feet" on doctrine and allow the consumer to have a very real understanding of this marvelous book. Rightly divided, I want to help the reader understand the Word of God for themselves, God's people.

I do not have PhD in Divinity, but even greater a reward is that I am sealed in Christ until the day of redemption. This writing is from me, a minister, to you, a minister. I encourage you to be a good steward of God's word. Be enriched and go enrich!

EPHESIANS BACKGROUND

1. **Ephesians**
   1. 6 chapters, 155 verses, and 3,022 words (KJV).
   2. 1 of the 9 epistles written by Paul to seven various churches. This excludes the pastoral epistles.
   3. These 9 letters can be divided as:
   - Salvation in Christ
     - Romans
     - 1 & 2 Corinthians
     - Galatians
   - Body of Christ
     - Ephesians
     - Philippians
     - Colossians
   - Coming of Christ
     - 1 & 2 Thessalonians
   - Together, these epistles make up the "form of sound words" (2 Timothy 1:13).

2. **Structure**

1. Conceptual structure:
   - Ephesians 1-3
     - Wealth, standing, calling, blessings, and riches
   - Ephesians 4-6
     - Walk, state, conduct, behavior, and responsibilities
2. Epistle structure:
   - 1:1-2, Salutation
   - 1:3-3:19, Doctrinal; as to our standing
   - 3:20-21; Doxology
   - 4:1-6:20, Doctrinal; as to our state
   - 6:21-24, Benediction

3. **Notes regarding the nature of Ephesians**

   1. "Ephesians is the second of the great textbooks of doctrinal instruction for believers in this Dispensation ["Age of Grace"] ~ E.W. Bullinger
   2. Bullinger describes Ephesians as behind Romans in this list. Romans establish the standing of the saint in Christ and the Gospel's effect. The epistle of Ephesians furthers this truth. Ephesians teaches that the sinner is now in God's sight and purpose sent.
   3. Romans ends in reference to the revelation of the mys-

tery, while Ephesians unfolds it.

4. Explains Jews and Gentiles are called out to be the Church and the Body of Christ (Key-note).

5. Unveils the "mystery" and the "Dispensation of the fullness of times."

- Glorifying Christ as the glorified head over the Body of Christ (Church).

- This glorious purpose was hidden in God and now Christ lives in each and every believer with His purpose unveiled.

6. The greater part of the Ephesians focusses on doctrine.

- One half has to do with standing, the other discusses our state.

4. Date: A.D. 61-62, possibly the end of 62

- According to Bishop Lightfoot, Ephesians was written as the epistle to the Philippians.

5. Title: To Ephesus

1. Note* In some early manuscripts, "At Ephesus", is not found. Some (not all) early Christian apologists do not mention Ephesus either (e.g. Origen, Basil).

- Various explanations state that some early manuscripts dismissed the location so that a particular church name could be written in. Regardless, it is obvious that this letter is written to a

Gentile audience.
- The letter is addressed to the saints at Ephesus and to the faithful in Christ.

6. **Ephesus background:**

- Great commercial center in Asia Minor (In now modern-day Turkey)
- Situated on the Cayster River, which comes out on the Aegean Sea
- Notable for the temple of Artemis (Diana), one of the wonders of the world (Acts 19:27)

7. **Author: The Apostle Paul** (Note* Liberal scholarship argues this.)

8. **Written from: Possibly written from Rome**

- Letter is delivered by a man name Tychicus (Ephesians 6:21-22).

EPHESIANS 1

1:1 Paul, an apostle of Jesus Christ by the will of God, to the saints which are at Ephesus, and to the faithful in Christ Jesus:

"Paul" is the first word of every epistle he authored. Often, Paul defended his position of apostleship early in the majority of his epistles. In this epistle, the pattern is reciprocated.

The pattern is of particular importance because of the constant scrutiny of false teachers and the distinctness of his ministry to the Gentiles.

A "saint" is anyone who has faith in Christ for their salvation. The term means "sanctified in Christ". This is synonymous with the "faithful in Christ".

Paul's ministry at Ephesus is detailed in Acts 18:19-19:41. The ministry that he began continued throughout his departure and he has even heard reports of it (v.15).

Pastor David Osteen reasons that "The faithful in Christ Jesus" is specifically mentioned because Paul is writing to the Spiritual saints versus the carnal saints at Corinth (1 Corinthians 2:1-8).

1:2 Grace be to you, and peace, from God our Father, and from the Lord Jesus Christ.

From God we receive grace and peace follows. Grace and peace are derived from the Gospel of Jesus Christ. Grace was included in all of Paul's salutations due to its importance within his message and also the cultural ties. "Grace" being a more common salutation of the Gentiles and "peace" being common for the Jews.

1:3 Blessed be the God and Father of our Lord Jesus Christ, who hath blessed us with all spiritual blessings in heavenly places in Christ:

Paul offers a blessing to God for blessing us with all Spiritual blessings. This is another pattern we should reciprocate (1 Corinthians 11:1). A lot of times, we hear of people desperately seeking blessings as if we do not already possess *all* of them. Verses 3-14 highlights quite a few of these blessings. These blessings are from the Father, through Christ, by the Holy Spirit who abides in us. Remember [Will~Father; Work~Son; Witness~Spirit].

We are blessed with all Spiritual blessings at the moment of salvation and rely on the hope and trust that they are in "Heavenly places", not on Earth.

These blessings are based on our *position* in Christ.

1:4 According as he hath chosen us in him before the foundation of the world, that we should be holy and without blame before him in love:

We are chosen in Christ. God's will is for all to be saved and blameless in Christ (1 Timothy 2:4). All are chosen; however, the prize needs to be accepted. When we believe in Christ's finished work, there is a position change. From the first Adam (Originated in Adam's sin) to the second Adam (Righteousness offered by Christ) (Romans 5:12-18).

The chosen in Christ has nothing to do with being predestined to salvation, but rather the saints being predestined unto glory when they believe in the Gospel. We have the will to believe in His Gospel.

Providentially, God has chosen life for all before the foundation of the World. The nature of the 1st Adam works to oppose this plan.

Not only does the first Adam (flesh) oppose this plan, but the dark rulers of the world, particularly, the Devil (Ephesians 6:11-12).

1:5 Having predestinated us unto the adoption of children by Jesus Christ to himself, according to the good pleasure of his will

[Predestined] Check note 1:4

Adoption in this sense, has a lot more to do with standing, than in what is often interpreted. It is often interpreted in the sense of displacement from one situation into another family. This does happen upon salvation and we become part of the family of God. Our adoption has a lot to do with position and the fullness of our sonship in Christ. This position comes with many privileges and responsibilities (Ephesians 1:3-14; Galatians 4:1-7).

One more note regarding predestination. The concept of predestination is to God and the act of His pre-chosen of all humanity is truly only by His graciousness. His grace made this act "according to the good pleasure of His will" (v.5).

1:6 To the praise of the glory of his grace, wherein he hath made us accepted in the beloved.

It is by God's grace that we are accepted. The "beloved" noted in this verse is God's beloved son, Jesus Christ.

We are accepted because of Christ. Being in Christ is our standing.

Praise God for His beautiful will and the "glory of His grace".

1:7 In whom we have redemption through his blood, the forgiveness of sins, according to the riches of his grace

Redemption is when something or someone has been bought with a price. God redeemed us from our sins with the high price of the blood of His Son Jesus Christ. Without Christ's perfect sacrifice and blood, redemption from our past, present, and future sins (Colossians 2:13) would not be possible.

In verse 6, Paul refers to the "glory of His grace". In verse 7, Paul refers to the "riches of His grace". Being identified and positioned in Christ, gives us access to the glory and wealth of God's grace (Ephesians 3:8).

1:8-10 Wherein he hath abounded toward us in all wisdom and prudence;

Having made known unto us the mystery of his will, according to his good pleasure which he hath purposed in himself:

That in the dispensation of the fulness of times he might gather together in one all things in Christ, both which are in heaven, and which are on earth; even in him:

*Due to the importance of the concept, I would like to work through these verses briefly, as a whole. There may be varying and or contrary views regarding these verses.

The mystery is not an "off-the-cuff" concept formulated by God. It was hidden by Him, in Him, and although components of it were prophesied, to what extent was unknown.

Romans 16:25 exemplifies the mystery being kept since the world began by God.

Knowing the mystery is one of the Spiritual blessings mentioned within the list created in Ephesians 1:3-14. This mystery is concerning "the dispensation of the fulness of times." The Bible explains that through the fall of the Jews, salvation came of the Gentiles (non-Jews) (Romans 11:11-15).

Through this fall, we live in the "Dispensation (Age) of Grace (God)" (Ephesians 3:2-13). With this Dispensation, Paul carried the special office of minister to the Gentile, who by revelation of God was able to deliver the mystery (Romans 11:13-15; Ephesians 3:1-9; Colossians 1:25).

The mystery was kept a mystery until unveiled in God's perfect time and will. That Christ would come, die, be buried, and rise again, to ascend, only to return in the Holy Spirit to dwell in man (Colossians 1:27) in the Dispensation of Grace. Within the Dispensation of Grace, we become a part of the Body of Christ and are given a Heavenly inheritance.

This changes our position from the 1st Adam to the 2nd Adam (In Christ) no longer need the circumcision of the Jewish faith to join the family of God.

*This will be discussed more particularly in the study on Ephesians 3 with the *fellowship of the mystery.*

1:11 In whom also we have obtained an inheritance, being predestinated according to the purpose of him who worketh all things after the counsel of his own will:

Prior to the Dispensation of Grace, the glorious inheritance that the Jews possessed from God was foreign to the Gentiles. Now, every member of the Body of Christ has a Heavenly inheritance (Colossians 3:24). This is all in God's perfect will.

1:12-13 That we should be to the praise of his glory, who first trusted in Christ.

In whom ye also trusted, after that ye heard the word of truth, the gospel of your salvation: in whom also after that ye believed, ye were sealed with that holy Spirit of promise

Humanity's purpose of living is to glorify God. When believing in Christ and depending on His finished work and Gospel, we reflect Christ's evident glory. From here, our lives are a sacrifice and praise of Him (Romans 12:1-2).

Our salvation is in Jesus Christ (1 Corinthians 15:3-4). When we believe, we are justified. When justified, we are sealed in the "Holy Spirit of promise". Belief comes with an aspect of trust in our salvation and this sealing is our eternal security.

At the moment of salvation a few things happen:

1. Circumcision (Of the heart, blameless)(Colossians 2:13)
2. Regenerates (Titus 3:5)
3. Baptizes (Colossians 2:12)
4. Indwells (1 Corinthians 3:16)
5. Seals (Ephesians 1:13; 4:30)

1:14 Which is the earnest of our inheritance until the redemption of the purchased possession, unto the praise of his glory.

The first fruits of the Spirit is the life we are living in Christ

(Romans 8:23) and the earnestness of our inheritance is life in Christ until the redemption of our glorified bodies in Heaven. Once again, being all for His glory.

1:15-16 Wherefore I also, after I heard of your faith in the Lord Jesus, and love unto all the saints

Cease not to give thanks for you, making mention of you in my prayers

Paul often reflected on his thankfulness for the testimonies and faiths of other believers. This is a pattern within the writings of the Apostle Paul. This pattern is shown to be conducted by Paul here and the pattern is likewise encouraged in Philippians 4:6 and 1st Corinthians 11:1.

Chapter 1 can be divided into two sections. The 1st section already discussed pertaining to the Spiritual blessings (v.1-14). The 2nd half pertains to the blessings impact on the Church. It is notable that obtaining the blessings is not Paul's prayer, but rather realizing that as saints we already have them.

Not realizing this truth leaves Christians seeking and in a constant state of spiritual fear and turmoil.

Additionally, the two prayers within Chapter 1 are about the Spiritual knowledge of truth and realization of the truth we possess in Christ.

1:17-19 That the God of our Lord Jesus Christ, the Father of glory, may give unto you the spirit of wisdom and revelation in the knowledge of him:

The eyes of your understanding being enlightened; that ye may know what is the hope of his calling, and what the riches of the glory of his inheritance in the saints

And what is the exceeding greatness of his power to us-ward who believe, according to the working of his mighty power

Paul's prayer is addressed to the "God of our Lord Jesus Christ, the father of glory". This address denotes God as the originator of glory.

The word for "glory" here is "doxa" in the original Greek writing. Vine's Expository Dictionary defines the term in various ways; however, essentially represents God's self-manifestation of Himself, which is divine, splendorous, and perfect. God is the origin of such traits.

As in verse 17, it is only by God that we obtain wisdom and truth about Him. This makes perfect sense, as no one would know God better. This knowledge is revealed by the Spirit (1 Corinthians 2:1-16).

God graciously supplies the believer with understanding and knowledge of the blessings we receive in Christ. The question is, will we believe them also?

Nonetheless, as ministers of the Gospel, it is not our job to know ourselves better; however, rather know Him better. With this task, we can not be steered wrong considering our identity is in Him (Philiphians 3:10; Romans 8:1).

There is hope in the calling of Christ. This is essentially the hope of the saint because the Body of Christ is a called-out collection of individuals. We as the Church have the hope of the inheritance of Heaven through the Gospel of Christ (Titus 2:13)!

1:20-23 Which he wrought in Christ, when he raised him from the dead, and set him at his own right hand in the heavenly places,

Far above all principality, and power, and might, and dominion, and every name that is named, not only in this world, but also in that which is to come:

And hath put all things under his feet, and gave him to be the head over all things to the church

Which is his body, the fulness of him that filleth all in all.

Once again, Paul sets the believers' sight on "heavenly places" rather than the broken, fragile promises of the world (v.20).

The mighty power of Christ is and has been eternal; and was worked in Christ through His resurrection which allowed the justification and intercession of man (Romans 4:25; 1 Corinthians 15:13-15).

Importantly, Christ's authority surpasses all power and rulership in the physical and spiritual realms. This is what we proclaim when announcing that "Jesus is Lord". He is the highest power.

As the Church and the Body of Christ, Jesus is the head of operations. His mighty power is manifested in us Spiritually and we possess His resurrection power (Romans 6:3-4).

EPHESIANS 2

2:1-3 And you hath he quickened, who were dead in trespasses and sins;

Wherein in time past ye walked according to the course of this world, according to the prince of the power of the air, the spirit that now worketh in the children of disobedience:

Among whom also we all had our conversation in times past in the lusts of our flesh, fulfilling the desires of the flesh and of the mind; and were by nature the children of wrath, even as others.

Chapter 1 of Ephesians primarily deals with the Spiritual possessions of a Christian. Chapter 2 of the epistle has much to do with the position of a Christian within the Body of Christ.

The comparison could also be represented as *benefits* versus *how to* knowledge (Or better yet, what has already been done by Jesus).

Quicken: A now unfortunately archaic term that simply means "to make alive" or to "preserve alive".

Chapter 2 follows chapter 1 where the authority and power of Christ is expounded upon. It is only by Christ's grace, power, and Gospel that we can be *quickened* and made alive.

When alive in Christ, remembering where we were rescued from fortifies thanksgiving (Corinthians 11:2; Titus 3:1-7).

Regarding the flesh, there is nothing positive to note in the Bible about our conflicting carnal nature. It is important to note that the righteousness of God surpasses it.

It is by Christ's power and loving kindness that while we are yet immersed in wickedness, He alone has the power to pull us up out of the miry clay of sin.

Romans 5:8 states,

"But God commendeth his love toward us, in that, while we were yet sinners, Christ died for us."

In the lives of the lost, there are three harmful forces mentioned within verses 1 to 3: The world, the Devil, and the flesh.

Succumbing to these forces is habitual for Christians and the lost alike. This does not dismiss Biblical guidance through the help of the Spirit to curve unrighteousness.

In Christ however, we are counted as blameless according to His imputed righteousness (Romans 8:1; Ephesians 1:4; Philiphians 2:15).

2:4-9 But God, who is rich in mercy, for his great love wherewith he loved us,

Even when we were dead in sins, hath quickened us together with Christ, (by grace ye are saved;)

And hath raised us up together, and made us sit together in heavenly places in Christ Jesus:

That in the ages to come he might shew the exceeding riches of his grace in his kindness toward us through Christ Jesus.

For by grace are ye saved through faith; and that not of your-selves: it is the gift of God:

Not of works, lest any man should boast.

Paul is speaking communally regarding the Body of Christ, the Church.

He explains that God is "rich in mercy" provoked by Christ's great love for us.

The Greek word here for mercy is *eleos*. Vine's Expository Diction-ary of New Testament Words explains this term as an "outward manifestation of pity".

Vine goes on to state that grace is the loving attitude of God to the rebel. Mercy is the act of grace. Peace is the resulting experience in the heart of man.

God is rich in mercy. He has unlimited wealth.

While we were still in sin, Christ died for us (Romans 5:8). While dead in sin, Christ made us alive [5].

Our position is one of a Heavenly calling and far superior to any-thing this Earth has to offer. Pastor David Osteen describes our position as "...trophies of His grace".

Chapter 2 lays out that we are saved by grace through faith. This grace is a free gift offered simply through belief in God's Son.

2:10 For we are his workmanship, created in Christ Jesus unto good works, which God hath before ordained that we should walk in them.

We are God's workmanship and are created for a purpose. The good works depicted serve the purpose of glorifying God (Isaiah 43:7). Good works are not a means of salvation so do not get this confused.

Good works are the fruit and byproduct of the new creation that God makes through the work of the Holy Spirit and the Gospel of Jesus Christ.

Our works can not be deemed "good" without a relationship with Jesus Christ. The Word of God states that when someone is in the flesh, they cannot please God (Romans 8:8-9).

2:11-12 Wherefore remember, that ye being in time past Gentiles in the flesh, who are called Uncircumcision by that which is called the Circumcision in the flesh made by hands;

That at that time ye were without Christ, being aliens from the commonwealth of Israel, and strangers from the covenants of promise, having no hope, and without God in the world:

Paul calls Gentile Christians to a time of remembrance. He calls them to remember when their position was not in Christ but was rather in the flesh.

Prior to the finished work of Christ's Gospel, salvation was ascertained by circumcision and works.

The Apostle Paul is reminding the Gentiles to remember the time prior to their salvation where they could be referred to as uncircumcised (Gentiles) by the circumcised (Jews).

Gentiles were isolated from the promises and blessings from God to Israel. This isolation left them with no hope.

This is exemplified through Matthew 10:5-6 when Jesus instructs His disciples to go *not* into the way of Gentiles; but, rather focus themselves on the nation of Israel.

2:13-18 But now in Christ Jesus ye who sometimes were far off are made nigh by the blood of Christ.

For he is our peace, who hath made both one, and hath broken down the middle wall of partition between us;

Having abolished in his flesh the enmity, even the law of commandments contained in ordinances; for to make in himself of twain one new man, so making peace;

And that he might reconcile both unto God in one body by the cross, having slain the enmity thereby:

And came and preached peace to you which were afar off, and to them that were nigh.

For through him we both have access by one Spirit unto the Father.

We are offered the spiritual power of Christ's Gospel through His completed work. This is once again referring to the position change and placement into the Body of Christ.

Christ's blood ended isolation for everyone and instituted the Body of Christ. Christ created this one body [v.14] by tearing down the spiritual wall that divided Jew and Gentile.

When this wall was torn down, it was in this Body that Paul states that, "There is neither Jew nor Greek, there is neither bond nor free, there is neither male nor female: for ye are all one in Christ Jesus."

And if ye be Christ's, then are ye Abraham's seed, and heirs according to the promise" (Galatians 3:28-29).

This marvelous creation is what we deem "The Church." Not a building. Not the thing that an offering plate funds. The Body of Christ is *The Church.*

In the church, peace is made by way of placement into His body and He stands as our intercessor. This makes the right relationship with God possible.

Ephesians 2:15 defeats the basis for replacement theology. The Church does not become the "New Israel" after Christ's Gospel is established. Jew and Gentile distinctions are removed upon belief in His Gospel.

Differences are reconciled within the Body of Christ which stands as a "new man".

A new man refers to the Church, a unique institution to Israel (Although the Gospel is rooted and derived from). It also refers to the "new creation" (2 Corinthians 5:17) and the "new man" that is put on from renewal of true knowledge of Christ (Colossians 3:10).

Therefore, the new man can refer to *the* Church and the adherents that make up the Body of Christ.

Lastly, verse 18 shows the unity of the Trinity in how Christ (The Son) gives us access through the Holy Spirit to the Father.

2:19-22 Now therefore ye are no more strangers and foreigners, but fellowcitizens with the saints, and of the household of God;

And are built upon the foundation of the apostles and prophets, Jesus Christ himself being the chief corner stone;

In whom all the building fitly framed together groweth unto an holy temple in the Lord:

In whom ye also are builded together for an habitation of God through the Spirit.

Christ is the foundation and the cornerstone of our faith. A cornerstone is traditionally the first stone laid and the most significant with the construction of an institution.

Jesus is the foundation of our faith. By Him, we are allowed sainthood (sanctification) upon the acceptance of His Gospel and membership into the family of God.

Christ being the cornerstone of our faith also sets the distinctiveness of preeminence. That He has always been and was before the apostles and prophets from which our faith is derived.

EPHESIANS 3

3:1-2 For this cause I Paul, the prisoner of Jesus Christ for you Gentiles

If ye have heard of the dispensation of the grace of God which is given me to you-ward

This chapter division begins by Paul addressing the cause (reasoning) behind his message.

He says "for this cause," after chapter 2 ends with him discussing the coagulation (joining) of the Christian church and family of God.

Also, when Paul refers to himself as a prisoner, he is jointly addressing his standing. He is a captive of Jesus Christ.

This is not the only time that Paul (And other Biblical writers) boasts this title. Paul begins Chapter 4 of Ephesians with this title as well as it being found in Philemon, Timothy, Hebrews, etc.

His target audience is also addressed through this first verse. Christ's captivity placed a purpose in his life as well. To share *the* Gospel and *the* mystery with the Gentiles.

Paul's purpose and ministry was to the Gentiles. He delivered the knowledge of the "dispensation of the grace of God." The age that we live within now, living fully and freely within the grace that God supplied through the Gospel of Jesus Christ.

Verse 2 of Ephesians 3 is essentially important as we see that the beginning of this age came from the revelation that Jesus Christ directly delivered to Paul (Ephesians 3:3; Galatians 1:12).

3:3-6 How that by revelation he made known unto me the mystery; (as I wrote afore in few words,

Whereby, when ye read, ye may understand my knowledge in the mystery of Christ)

Which in other ages was not made known unto the sons of men, as it is now revealed unto his holy apostles and prophets by the Spirit;

That the Gentiles should be fellowheirs, and of the same body, and partakers of his promise in Christ by the gospel:

[Verse 3 reference 3:2]

From this revelation, Paul is to deliver his knowledge of Christ's revelation to the Body of Christ, particularly the Gentiles.

This revelation (The Mystery of Christ) was not known in any other age [time] or group of people. If it was to be prophesied, it would contradict the words of Paul in Romans 16:25, 2 Timothy 1:9, Galatians 1:12, and Ephesians 3:9

The "holy apostles and prophets by the Spirit" is referring to the apostles and prophets after the cross and during the time of Paul. We see this through the context of the situation and the phrase "as it is now revealed."

However, the primary catalyst of this message being propelled is not man. It is done "by the Spirit."

The three proponents of the mystery of Christ is that the Gentiles:

- Are fellow heirs, with Christ and his eternal inheritance. As fellow heirs we will be glorified as Jesus is in Heaven (Romans 8:17).

- Are of the same body [The Body of Christ]. We are a new creation and *not* a continuation of Israel (1 Corinthians 12:13). The Body of Christ is an entity within the age of grace. Distinctions were torn down and all who believe in the Gospel of Jesus Christ are part of The Body [The Church] (Review notes for Ephesians 1:22-23).

- Are partakers of the promise in Christ by the Gospel (Grace/ Salvation). Christ's work finished at the Cross and followed by His salvation allowed a way to right relationship with God (1 Corinthians 15:3-4). Christ promised through His grace that we can be saved and receive His Holy Spirit.

3:7-9 Whereof I was made a minister, according to the gift of the grace of God given unto me by the effectual working of His power.

Unto me, who am less than the least of all saints, is this grace given, that I should preach among the Gentiles the unsearchable riches of Christ;

And to make all men see what is the fellowship of the mystery, which from the beginning of the world hath been hid in God, who created all things by Jesus Christ:

Paul is undoubtedly the minister to the Gentiles, carrying the mystery by the grace of God.

He was appointed by Christ to be an apostolic minister by the grace of God. Grace being the means by which God operates.

(Romans 11:13; 15:15-16).

Paul's office is magnified and the effectual working of His power pertains to the power that Paul wielded in the Holy Spirit who (like us) was with Paul constantly. We see an example of this in Acts 15:12.

Paul addresses himself as the "least of all saints" because of his role in the persecution of the Church (1 Corinthians 15:9-10).

Despite this, in 1 Corinthians 15:10, Paul defends that he has laboured more than all of the saints by the grace of God.

Least does *not* mean behind any saints. His role is a very special appointment.

The "unsearchable riches of Christ" are already our inheritance when we are saved and sealed. These parallel with the "spiritual blessings in heavenly places in Christ" (Ephesians 1:3).

They are not Earthly riches as the Israelites sought, but rather one unseen at this time, that is still to come. Paul preached these riches to the Gentiles.

Paul's preaching was his way of communicating important truths (Romans 10:14-15). Paul set out to teach fellowship within the Body of Christ. Fellowship being by way of the Spirit (2 Corinthians 13:14).

A truth that has been hidden *in* God (The Creator) since the "beginning of the world."

3:10-12 To the intent that now unto the principalities and powers in heavenly places might be known by the church the manifold wisdom of God,

According to the eternal purpose which he purposed in Christ Jesus our Lord:

In whom we have boldness and access with confidence by the faith of him.

God's intention is to reveal this Heavenly wisdom and knowledge (manifold knowledge) to the Church.

This is and has been the eternal purpose that God had through the effectual working of Jesus Christ. The Church is not a plan B kind of situation.

Christ supplied fellowship with Him and the Body of Christ. He made a way so that we can approach God confidently and securely. This is not through works, but rather by grace through faith.

3:13 Wherefore I desire that ye faint not at my tribulations for you, which is your glory.

Firstly, I love what Pastor David Osteen has to say about it. He wrote that "Christ suffered to purchase our salvation and Paul suffered to proclaim it" (Colossians 1:24).

Paralleling this verse with Colossians 1:24, we see that Paul had experienced great tribulation and afflictions for the sake of the Body of Christ.

Just as he did not let trials reduce his zeal for the Gospel, he encourages the Church to remain strong in light of his tribulations as well.

3:14-15 For this cause I bow my knees unto the Father of our Lord Jesus Christ,

Of whom the whole family in heaven and earth is named

Throughout the Bible, bowing down is an act of humble worship (ex. Exodus 20:5; Psalm 95:6; Philippians 2:10).

When we go to the Father in prayer, we are praying to the Father in the name of the Lord Jesus Christ (Ephesians 5:20) by the Holy Spirit.

Christians are all part of the family of God on Earth and in Heaven (Galatians 3:26).

Additionally, Jesus Christ is the intercessor of our prayers to the Father and because of this we can humbly approach Him in prayer (Romans 8:34).

3:16 That he would grant you, according to the riches of his glory, to be strengthened with might by his Spirit in the inner man

We are strengthened by the Spirit in the inner man by the Word of God.

Colossians 3:16 reads,

"Let the word of Christ dwell in you richly in all wisdom; teaching and admonishing one another in psalms and hymns and spiritual songs, singing with grace in your hearts to the Lord."

Also, the inner man needs to be a definitive focus within our prayer because it is an eternal matter, not the outward man.

3:17-19 That Christ may dwell in your hearts by faith; that ye, being rooted and grounded in love

May be able to comprehend with all saints what is the breadth, and length, and depth, and height;

And to know the love of Christ, which passeth knowledge, that ye might be filled with all the fulness of God.

Christ dwells in the heart of the believers and it is possible by faith (Colossians 1:27).

Moreover, Christ dwelling in us means that we do not have to pray for the presence of God or for His Spirit to continuously descend upon us as it did in early Acts.

Whereas we do not live from experience to experience; rather, we stand and live in faith and constant communion with the Holy Spirit.

Like a structure under attack by an earthquake, we as Christians can stay solid and standing by the love of God.

When grounded in love, we have an extraordinary ability offered only by the Holy Spirit. We are able to know the love of Christ.

The Word says that this love "passeth knowledge." With our human knowledge we will not be able to know this love.

However, we know it by the Spirit, (Romans 5:5), which is delivered through the mystery that Paul delivered (Ephesians 3:3-6).

This Spiritual knowledge is important living what some would deem the "full" Christian life. A full Christian life requires "all the fulness of God" which comes by believing in His Gospel (1 Corinthians 15:3-4).

3:20-21 Now unto him that is able to do exceeding abundantly

above all that we ask or think, according to the power that worketh in us,

Unto him be glory in the church by Christ Jesus throughout all ages, world without end. Amen.

Lastly, with verse 21, the book of Ephesians is divided in half and the main doctrinal portion is concluded.

Undoubtedly, it is concluded with the full assurance that God is not limited in His mighty works. The power that we pray to and draw from is already inside of each and every believer.

It is His Holy Spirit. The Spirit of Christ Jesus reflects the glory of Christ through His Body (The Church). This will be true, endlessly into eternity.

EPHESIANS 4

4:1 I therefore, the prisoner of the Lord, beseech you that ye walk worthy of the vocation wherewith ye are called

Beginning in Chapter 4, Paul redirects his attention from primarily doctrinal to primarily practical. This is our state currently as Christians and how to practically live out our faith.

He begins by referring to himself as a captive of the Lord. He is sealed by the Spirit as a consequence (positive consequence) to his belief in the Gospel of Jesus Christ (Ephesians 1:13-14).

His position is in the Body of Christ and his state was as a prisoner.

Paul uses other strong language when referring to his present state that carries similar connotations. An example of this is in Romans 1 when Paul refers to himself as a "servant of Jesus Christ".

The word Paul utilizes here, *doulos*, can be accurately described as a "slave" or "bondman" as well. Regardless, Paul clearly indicates that he has a master and that his master is Jesus Christ.

It is also worth noting once more, a difference between law and grace. The law is filled with hundreds of commandments while Paul's teaching of grace beseeches (pleas) what we "ought to" do (ex. Romans 15:1, 1 Corinthians 9:10).

Paul uses the word "beseech" 23 times within his epistles.

All fear is gone when abiding in Christ. Even in our failures,

Christ's imputed righteousness covers us.

This is not a reason to go on living in sin (Romans 6:1-2), though it is a reason to rejoice. We have been free from a law that no man (except Christ) could ever keep.

Walking worthy of the vocation means to walk worthy of the calling that Christ has placed on our life.

The nature of this high (Philippians 3:14) and holy (2 Timothy 1:9) calling is a matter first dealt with by Paul in Ephesians 4.

4:2-3 With all lowliness and meekness, with longsuffering, forbearing one another in love;

Endeavouring to keep the unity of the Spirit in the bond of peace.

These two verses describe how the Body of Christ is to operate and treat each other. We are to fellowship with the Body first of all in Spirit and in truth.

Practically, this presents itself in a humble and patient love. Unity of the Spirit (fellowship) is kept strong in peace. Saying this, unity should be a priority within the Body of Christ.

4:4-6 There is one body, and one Spirit, even as ye are called in one hope of your calling;

One Lord, one faith, one baptism,

One God and Father of all, who is above all, and through all, and in you all.

Following unity, Paul presents a list of things that are unified within our faith. These three verses in themselves can have a comprehensive commentary describing the topics listed.

However, we shall conduct an overview of these topics.

The Body is not referring to our individual bodies, but the Body of Christ (Ephesians 1:23, Romans 12:5).

The Spirit is referring to the Holy Spirit that indwells in the heart of each believer and seals them within the Body of Christ.

The hope of our calling is the single solitary hope that we share within the Body of Christ.

The hope of glory, Christ in us (Colossians 1:27) is the only hope that can secure us (The Body of Christ) as fellow heirs (Ephesians 3:6) with Christ.

Looking ahead, the one baptism referred to is a spiritual baptism into the Body of Christ (1 Corinthians 12:13). This is a component of the mystery that Paul refers to continuously and is something that God kept hidden (Romans 16:25).

This one baptism is the component that unites all Christian into a fellowship.

It is a glorious hope and a high, holy calling.

We have one Lord, composed of the Holy Trinity, and by the Gospel of Jesus Christ our faith is solely in our Lord as salvation.

Here Paul is not referring to a generic faith; rather, he is referring to *The Faith* (Philippians 1:27) by *The Gospel*.

Lastly, God has authority above all, that is manifested in all of us by the Spirit, and carried out through Christians who carry the Word with them.

Our source of Godly power is derived from His sacred Word.

4:7 But unto every one of us is given grace according to the measure of the gift of Christ.

Note the word, "But". There is a difference from the prior few verses. There is *not* one grace.

This is not a shared grace, as each of us is given a measure of grace as a gift from Christ (Ex. Ephesians 3:7).

Grace is how God operates in our time and although omnipresent, deals with each of us on an individual level when we come into the right relationship with Him. This is done by His grace.

Whenever God gives humanity gifts, we are called to do something with it. Whether that is to edify, preach, teach, or serve, we have power to carry out the task (Romans 12:3-5).

4:8-11 Wherefore he saith, When he ascended up on high, he led captivity captive, and gave gifts unto men.

(Now that he ascended, what is it but that he also descended first into the lower parts of the earth?

He that descended is the same also that ascended up far above all heavens, that he might fill all things.)

And he gave some, apostles; and some, prophets; and some, evangelists; and some, pastors and teachers.

By the grace of God we are able to fulfill our roles and ministries within the Body of Christ.

Unity, as mentioned earlier in Ephesians, does not deflect from the importance of Biblical diversity. Diversity, not as the worldly flesh teaches, but in our ministries being carried out according to the measure of grace allotted.

As for gifts, this often becomes the focus of "diversity," yet this Scripture cannot be justification for such gifts. In the time that Paul wrote Ephesians, apostolic gifts and even prophecy was still prevalent.

There was a transition period between the Kingdom of Israel program and the Grace program we live in today.

However, the apostolic gifts have ceased (1 Corinthians 13:8-13) and are unnecessary in light of the completion of the Canon.

Many of Paul's apostolic gifts even ceased (ex. [Healing] Philippians 2:25-30).

They were foundational (Ephesians 2:20); yet God's completed Word stands as our ultimate authority now and extra-Biblical revelation is no true revelation at all.

A man of God is made perfect by the Gospel, which is of the Scripture/Word of God (2 Timothy 3:16-17). The Canon is completely capable of guiding successful ministry.

Some ministries have been specifically kept in operation; however, without some of the more notable apostolic gifts, these ministries may look different (ex. Pastor, teacher).

As for verses 9 and 10, note the contrast between Christ's descension into Hell (1 Peter 3:18-20) and then ascension to Heaven. Christ's glory has been at both ends. Above all principalities and powers, Christ is exalted (Ephesians 1:19-23).

4:12-16 For the perfecting of the saints, for the work of the min-

istry, for the edifying of the body of Christ:

Till we all come in the unity of the faith, and of the knowledge of the Son of God, unto a perfect man, unto the measure of the stature of the fulness of Christ:

That we henceforth be no more children, tossed to and fro, and carried about with every wind of doctrine, by the sleight of men, and cunning craftiness, whereby they lie in wait to deceive;

But speaking the truth in love, may grow up into him in all things, which is the head, even Christ:

From whom the whole body fitly joined together and compacted by that which every joint supplieth, according to the effectual working in the measure of every part, maketh increase of the body unto the edifying of itself in love.

Nonetheless, for verse 12, the roles that Paul listed strike an uncanny semblance to a verse mentioned earlier in this study.

2 Timothy 3:17 states that by inspired Scripture, man may "be perfect, thoroughly furnished unto all good works."

In verse 12, Paul places responsibility on the roles such as teachers, preachers, prophets, and apostles to teach the Word of God "for the perfecting of the saints".

Teachers do not perfect saints, the message they carried does.

God's word teaches that doctrine reproofs, corrects, instructs (2 Timothy 3:16), perfects, and edifies (Builds up) the Body of Christ.

Verses 12-16 are one complete sentence combined and concern ministry and its varying functions.

- Purpose is: Perfecting (v.12)
- Goal is (v.13-14): Unity of *The* Faith and knowledge of Christ raises us from babies in faith to adults (1 Corinthians 14:20) in the fullness of Christ Jesus.

Note what doctrine and knowledge we are raised up in matters (v.14). Anything other than doctrine derived from the true Gospel is deceiving and needs to be marked and avoided (Romans 16:17-18).

Failure to do such is why local Christian fellowships get ripped apart and unity of the Spirit is divided.

Paul has strong words for deceivers, who teach another Gospel. He states to "let him [them] be accursed" (Galatians 1:8-9).

- Motive is: Love (v.15-16)

Truth in love is the fertilizer of Christian growth.

Accurate Biblical love edifies the Body and makes a more effective movement for the Body of Christ. It is the first of the fruit of the Spirit for good reason and should be our motivation as we carry the head of the Body, Jesus Christ, in our life.

4:17-19 This I say therefore, and testify in the Lord, that ye henceforth walk not as other Gentiles walk, in the vanity of their mind,

Having the understanding darkened, being alienated from the

life of God through the ignorance that is in them, because of the blindness of their heart:

Who being past feeling have given themselves over unto lasciviousness, to work all uncleanness with greediness.

Paul's general audience is once again addressed in verse 17 when he states, "As other Gentiles walk." In Romans 11:13, Paul refers to himself as the apostle to the Gentiles and in this statement he magnifies his office.

He states through most of his epistles that we should "walk worthy" (ex. Colossians 1:10-14). This pattern is kept *and* he continues to address how this walk should look; particularly to the Gentiles.

It is important to note that this instruction is given "in the Lord." This instruction is not something that Paul devised. This message is from the Lord through the apostle Paul.

Vanity of mind refers to a mind without any substance. It could be noted that faith is the substance of things hoped for and evidence of things not seen (Hebrews 11:1).

An ignorant mind has little to no faith in God.

Ignorance alienates us from God. In contrast, belief and the knowledge of the truth (**1 Timothy 2:4**) which is in Christ Jesus, brings us into the family of God. Alienation to family is a big jump on a big spectrum that is allowed by the big work of a big God.

This amazing work echos the words of our beautiful Savior in John 8:32,

"And ye shall know the truth, and the truth shall make you free."

Free from sin. Free from death. Free from the crooked and un-worthy walk that humanity brandishes prior to the transforming work of Christ.

Prior to salvation, the heart is blind and works on autopilot. This autopilot is set to carry out fleshly desires.

Nonetheless, Christ saves us from these corrupting desires through His righteousness and grace.

This is partly what it means to be "saved from ourselves", although God has saved us from so much and we should be grateful for it."

Ignorance leads to a searing of the mind; which can be charac-terized as God allowing people to "have at themselves" and be-come corrupted. Many times, this is the necessary pain that draws people to Christ and the hope He offers.

God does not inflict the pain, but rather allows people to have the sin they desperately want and desire. Often, this is a neces-sary condition to realizing what Christ's Gospel really is saving us from.

"Uncleanliness with greediness" refers to the nature of sin. Greediness was deduced by Ralph Waldo Trine as the "root of all error, sin, and crime, and that ignorance is the basis for all selfish-ness."

While Trine is not the Bible, his statement is impeccably true.

It would be difficult to think of any sin that does not have its root in selfishness. Often, ignorance of the effects of selfishness is what rationalizes erratic and controlled sin in the mind of a person.

4:20-21 But ye have not so learned Christ;

If so be that ye have heard him, and have been taught by him, as the truth is in Jesus:

Quite simply, we learn of the character, work, and will of Christ through His Word. We learn to hear what He has said, learn what He would have us to learn, and (once again) come to the knowledge of the truth which is only found in Him and His Gospel.

Also, not all of what God has said can be found in the red letters of the Bible.

We can look to the Old Testament and that of the apostles; particularly to the apostle to the Gentiles (Us), Paul.

When Paul makes claims to receive revelation from Christ, that signifies that his message is from Christ and should be regarded as God's word (Galatians 1:12).

This is one of the many reasons Paul was very protective against the evil adulteration that heretics were trying to add into the Gospel of Jesus Christ (Galatians 1:8-9).

4:22-24 That ye put off concerning the former conversation the old man, which is corrupt according to the deceitful lusts;

And be renewed in the spirit of your mind;

And that ye put on the new man, which after God is created in righteousness and true holiness.

This portion of Ephesians is not intended to be confusing; nonetheless, it is often avoided and overlooked by Christians because of the terminology.

Paul frequently used terms representing "old" and "new" self to represent the struggle between flesh (old man) and Spirit (new man).

I say struggle, but do not fear. Christ has already defeated flesh for us (Romans 6:6) and there is now no condemnation due to us in the Body of Christ (Romans 8:1).

Putting on the new man is us living in the righteousness and holiness of Christ. When we equip the new man, we are transformed by the renewing of our minds.

As we grow in Christ, we are better equipped to pop down the nose of the old man as he attempts to rear his head back up into our lives. We no longer have to gratify fleshly desires and can progressively become more astute spiritually (Galatians 5:16).

4:25-32 Wherefore putting away lying, speak every man truth with his neighbour: for we are members one of another.

Be ye angry, and sin not: let not the sun go down upon your wrath:

Neither give place to the devil.

Let him that stole steal no more: but rather let him labour, working with his hands the thing which is good, that he may have to give to him that needeth.

Let no corrupt communication proceed out of your mouth, but that which is good to the use of edifying, that it may minister grace unto the hearers.

And grieve not the holy Spirit of God, whereby ye are sealed unto the day of redemption.

Let all bitterness, and wrath, and anger, and clamour, and evil

speaking, be put away from you, with all malice:

And be ye kind one to another, tenderhearted, forgiving one another, even as God for Christ's sake hath forgiven you.

In the last study we introduced the "old man" and the "new man." In this portion of chapter 4, we discuss what it looks like to put off the old man and put on the new man.

These verses contrast actions and characteristics of the old man with the actions and the characteristics of the new man.

The old man is a liar while the new man equips and pursues truth. Particularly with his neighbor.

Within the context, a neighbor is referring to another member within the Body of Christ. We see that truth is a key to unity within the Body of Christ.

Interestingly enough, this is not the only place within the book of Ephesians that we are instructed to put on truth. We will see in chapter 6 that we are instructed to girt our loins with truth!

Paul introduces a truth himself showing that being angry does not have to be a sin. In fact, there is a place for it when it is not derived from carnality; but rather, righteousness.

Matthew Henry refers to sinful anger as an "ungoverned passion". Who is it ungoverned by? Christ and His *truth*.

Furthermore, humanity developing wrath has never ended well, especially in the Bible (ex. Romans 12:19). Do not let the sun go down on it and burrow within the crevices of your heart where it will sharply try and contest the dwelling of the new man.

Do not give place to the Devil in this way. Our body is the temple of the Holy Spirit (1 Corinthians 6:19).

Verse 28 depicts a sequence of transformation.

Steal no longer, labor, receive the fruits of your labor, and then give to those who are in need.

It begins with sin and ends with righteousness. This is what putting on the new man practically accomplishes in the lives of a member of the Body of Christ.

Once again, putting on the new man has a multi-fold purpose. When Paul refers to communication, this means that someone is interacting with another person.

When we become Christians, we are to put away corrupt communications from our mouth and re-purpose our words for the building up of the Body. This is all to be done so that men can experience the grace of Christ Jesus and allow the Gospel to be our primary focus.

Verse 30 has been controversial with Christian circles and many interpretations have been offered. Oxford dictionary defines *grieve* as to "cause great distress to someone."

We grieve the Spirit when we defy the Holy Spirit within us. Particularly, in this case by allowing the old man to continue.

Our body is a temple for the Holy Spirit and this temple was bought at a price. God sealed us unto the day of redemption. We were bought by the literal and spiritual anguish of our Lord Jesus Christ (John 12:27).

This verse specifically affirms the doctrine of eternal security in very plain language.

We are instructed to glorify God in all that we do and anything contrary causes distress to the Spirit which dwells inside of us (1 Corinthians 6:19-20).

Moreover, in verse 31 Paul reviews the traits that are of the old man and grieve the Holy Spirit and instructs the Body of Christ to put these things away!

Rather, equip the new man, which is kind and forgiving; because in this way we follow the example of God himself who has forgiven us of all our sins and seals us within His Body.

EPHESIANS 5

5:1-2 Be ye therefore followers of God, as dear children;

And walk in love, as Christ also hath loved us, and hath given himself for us an offering and a sacrifice to God for a sweetsmelling savour.

Followers of God are significantly more than a mere imitator. The act of following involves a form of modeling system. As Gentiles, we have a very practical model. The Apostle Paul instructs the Corinthian church to "Be ye followers of me, even as I also am of Christ" (1 Corinthians 11:1). Similar statements are instructed twice more in the Epistles as well.

This is a very fortunate instruction included within the Bible; because as Christians there are many aspects of life that would be impossible to replicate. Christ was/is perfect, man is not.

Especially for the Gentiles, Paul provides a brilliant example of a transformed and sold-out life for Jesus.

Be followers of God. Use the model and examples He provided within His word for this pursuit.

Speaking of examples, we are instructed to walk in love. We as Christians have the Holy Spirit, so we have the capability to walk in the same love that Christ has for us!

His love was not held back. He gave His life so that we may share eternity with Him. It is a strong love that as Christians we are often characterized by the action of His ultimate submission to the Father.

This is reasonable as Christ Himself states, "Greater love hath no man than this, that a man lay down his life for his friends" (John 15:13).

The reference to the sweet-smelling savour refers to the pleasing of God through sacrifice (ex. Leviticus 1:9) with Christ being the ultimate sacrifice.

In Ephesians 5 alone, there are three primary descriptions for the Spirit-led walk. Beginning in chapter 4, the Apostle Paul begins to describe the practicalities of doctrine.

In chapter 5, he instructs *the* walk to be: In love, as children of light, and circumspectly.

5:3-5 But fornication, and all uncleanness, or covetousness, let it not be once named among you, as becometh saints;

Neither filthiness, nor foolish talking, nor jesting, which are not convenient: but rather giving of thanks.

For this ye know, that no whoremonger, nor unclean person, nor covetous man, who is an idolater, hath any inheritance in the kingdom of Christ and of God.

I once heard it noted that these three verses indicate sin in differing manifestations. Verse 3 being the works of sin, verse 4 being an indicator of the source (The heart; ex. Jeremiah 17:9), and verse 5 indicating the types of people that are committing the sin.

Each verse ends with a spiritual reason contrary to our Spiritual walk of why not to indulge.

Sin is not fitting for saints (which all believers are), it is not good, and outside of Christ we are worthy of wrath.

5:6-10 Let no man deceive you with vain words: for because of these things cometh the wrath of God upon the children of disobedience.

Be not ye therefore partakers with them.

For ye were sometimes darkness, but now are ye light in the Lord: walk as children of light is:

(For the fruit of the Spirit is in all goodness and righteousness and truth;)

Proving what is acceptable unto the Lord.

This verse does not stand as some benign test of our salvation. Paul discusses in the doctrinal portion of Ephesians that we are sealed in the Holy Spirit (**Ephesians 1:13**). Paul is not going to contradict himself here.

Yet, it does discuss responsibility with our position within the Body of Christ.

Listening to these "vain words" is against God's word and counterproductive to the edification and building up of the Body of Christ. They hinder our walk.

In Colossians 1:10, Paul encourages healthy spiritual growth and practical spiritual living.

He states "That ye might walk worthy of the Lord unto all pleasing, being fruitful in every good work, and increasing in the knowledge of God" (Colossians 1:10).

We are called to increase in the knowledge of God and these false teachers will only twist and decrease genuine spiritual upbringing.

Darkness and light are similar to other Pauline contrasts of flesh and Spirit, old man and new man, first Adam and second Adam, and so on. Darkness is a state of being that is totally illuminated by the smallest of lights.

God is a God of light and with the God of Light living within us. We are part of the family of God (Galatians 6:10) and we are regarded as children of light. We should walk as children of light. The light being His word (Psalm 119:130).

Children of light exemplify the fruits of the Spirit (Galatians 5:22-23). These are acceptable traits to God the Father. The Christian walk produces fruit.

5:11-14 And have no fellowship with the unfruitful works of darkness, but rather reprove them.

For it is a shame even to speak of those things which are done of them in secret.

But all things that are reproved are made manifest by the light: for whatsoever doth make manifest is light.

Wherefore he saith, Awake thou that sleepest, and arise from the dead, and Christ shall give thee light.

Chapter 5, verse 11 continues discussing the practicalities of the Christian walk; specifically, walking as children of light.

Verse 11, 12, and 13 discuss how to curve sin when living with the grace that Christ offers.

The pattern is: [11] No fellowship (Stop), [12] Don't speak of them

(Avoid), [13] Reprove (Correct).

It is worth noting that the end of this spiritual mending process is "reprove." In order to reprimand and correct sin, light must be shown on it [13]. As Christians, we live by the light of the Word of the God and His Word is the standard by which darkness is overcome by light (2 Timothy 3:16-17).

Here in these Scriptures we also see the nature by which sin manifests itself within the church and in the world. It occurs in darkness and is often done in secret.

This is why Paul warns in 2nd Timothy 3:6 about sins that "creep into houses." Sin creeps into churches, houses, and countries. It subtly stays as a guest and then suddenly, the flesh tries to institute itself as the head of household.

Like the works of the Spirit, the works of the flesh produce fruit. However, this fruit is rotten and should be avoided at all costs.

We were once dead in our sin; nonetheless, in Christ's resurrection, we can come alive and have life abundantly (Ephesians 2:5-6).

5:15-17 See then that ye walk circumspectly, not as fools, but as wise,

Redeeming the time, because the days are evil.

Wherefore be ye not unwise, but understanding what the will of the Lord is.

As Christians living out practical sanctification and transformation, focussing on what we are doing right by Scriptural standards can consequently correct the wicked, fleshly way.

Paul instructs the Christian to "walk circumspectly" which means to walk cautiously, with full awareness of the consequences of our actions.

A part of walking circumspectly is to "redeem the time." Continuing reading and understanding verse 16 in full context helps Christians to understand the full brevity of this charge.

The wise walk circumspectly and understand the will of God, which is to "have all men to be saved, and to come unto the knowledge of the truth" (1 Timothy 2:4).

If we understand what God desires for humanity and that the "days are evil" and contrary to His will, then we will live by redeeming the time.

Redeeming the time means that we live for the will of God, using the time that He has allotted us, sold out for the purpose of furthering the Gospel of Jesus Christ which saves.

We are not called to "redeem the culture" contrary to the modern-age, fleshly pseudo-gospels floating around. We are called to "redeem the time."

Today is the day of salvation (2 Corinthians 6:2).

5:18 And be not drunk with wine, wherein is excess; but be filled with the Spirit;

This verse has much to do with control. Drunkenness is fleshly and allows the flesh to control instead of the Spirit which fills us from the moment of salvation.

Stop, avoid, and correct. Put on the new man and put off the old man (Ephesians 4:22-24)!

5:19-21 Speaking to yourselves in psalms and hymns and spiritual songs, singing and making melody in your heart to the Lord;

Giving thanks always for all things unto God and the Father in the name of our Lord Jesus Christ;

Submitting yourselves one to another in the fear of God.

Verse 19 addresses conducting this "singing" from your heart to the Lord. This verse states nothing about praise bands or anything of the sort. Otherwise, it would *not* say "speaking to yourselves."

This melody is addressed from "your heart" to "the Lord."

It is an internal worship overflowing from the heart of a believing Christian to the God who deserves such praise. After all, the psalmist addresses such praise and thanksgiving to God as "good" (Psalm 92:1).

As an act of worship, we are instructed to submit! First to the Holy Trinity and then to others. In love, *our* will is not the priority. The priority is the loving will of God that we inherit as it was "shed abroad in our hearts by the Holy Ghosts" (Romans 5:5).

Living in His will calls us to simply: Love God, love others (Matthew 22:36-39; Romans 13:8-10). This is true Biblical submission.

So... stop, avoid, reprove and be enriched!

5:22-24 Wives, submit yourselves unto your own husbands, as unto the Lord.

For the husband is the head of the wife, even as Christ is the head of the church: and he is the saviour of the body.

Therefore as the church is subject unto Christ, so let the wives be to their own husbands in every thing.

Understanding this pericope of Scripture must be done within its proper context. It must be understood with the entirety of Paul's letter to Ephesus.

It is within its proper context that we understand that this is practical instruction for the walk according to the will of God (Ephesians 5:17).

Saying this, we would also see that overall instruction of chapter 5 is addressed to the Body of Christ, the Church (Ephesians 5:21). Beginning, in verse 22, Paul addresses marriage within the Body of Christ; firstly, speaking the wives.

Paul instructs the Godly wife to "submit" themselves unto their husbands. Submission does not mean suppression. The Greek word, *hypotasso*, denotes that someone yields or is subject to another power.

We begin to see a groundwork laid for a complementary relationship between man and woman/husband and wife at the words "to their own husbands". Husbands are their wives and wives are their husbands.

This covenant is not revered anymore within many cultures; yet God intended marriage to be this way for a number of reasons.

Submission of the self is a willing submission. The husband is instituted as the head of the woman as Christ is likewise the head of the church (1 Corinthians 11:3).

The question is often raised of why one should submit? The answer is simply that marriage is a joining of two persons. Becoming one person still only requires one head. Otherwise, marriage becomes a 2-headed monster that cannot function unto its own self.

God is not the author of confusion (1 Corinthians 14:33) and confusion is derived from a lack of order. Confusion is contrary to God's nature.

Fleshly desires seek to overturn Godly order; however, we can trust Christ and His Word to establish us (2 Corinthians 1:21).

As wives submit "in everything" their identity is practically expressed in oneness with their husband.

5:25-27 Husbands, love your wives, even as Christ also loved the church, and gave himself for it;

That he might sanctify and cleanse it with the washing of water by the word,

That he might present it to himself a glorious church, not having spot, or wrinkle, or any such thing; but that it should be holy and without blemish.

At verse 25, Paul begins to address husbands with their task within the bonds of marriage, which is love.

Paul instructs husbands to love their wives fervently like Christ gave love to the Church. Christ loved the Church and sacrificed Himself (John 19:11) willingly by full obedience to the Father. He did this so that we may be without blemish.

Husbands are to love and be living sacrifices for their wives. Being the head of their wife is not a power trip as often presented within secular culture and liberal "Christianity." It is a God-given responsibility for man to bear.

To make light of this responsibility, is to make light of God's will within marriage and His ordinances. In marriage, man and woman have the opportunity to grow in love and be edified in the way of Christ.

5:28-30 So ought men to love their wives as their own bodies. He that loveth his wife loveth himself.

For no man ever yet hated his own flesh; but nourisheth and cherisheth it, even as the Lord the church:

For we are members of his body, of his flesh, and of his bones.

As denotes likeness. Men are instructed to love their wives as their own bodies and care for them. "Loving well" requires a sacrifice and loving their wives well should exceed the love of self.

Good husbands edify, nourish, and appreciate their wives. Once again, Paul likens this love to the love of God for the Body of Christ.

5:31-33 For this cause shall a man leave his father and mother, and shall be joined unto his wife, and they two shall be one flesh.

This is a great mystery: but I speak concerning Christ and the church.

Nevertheless let every one of you in particular so love his wife even as himself; and the wife see that she reverence her husband.

In verse 31, Paul references law when he points back to Genesis 2:24. This is the origins of marriage, where Adam and Eve's marital bond conjoins them essentially as "one flesh."

This covenant between man and woman is referenced as a great mystery and the profound experience derived from it is a tool that can be used to preach the great mystery to where humanity can be: Fellow heirs with Christ, within the Body of Christ, as partakers of His eternal promise!

Submit and love are very similar in how they present themselves within marriage.

EPHESIANS 6

6:1-3 Children, obey your parents in the Lord: for this is right.

Honour thy father and mother; which is the first commandment with promise;

That it may be well with thee, and thou mayest live long on the earth.

Beginning chapter 6, Paul continues with very practical instruction according to the mystery of Christ.

He reiterated obedience to parents and even looked to the Old Testament to reference the fifth of the ten commandments. The fifth commandment being, "Honour thy father and thy mother: that thy days may be long upon the land which the Lord thy God giveth thee."

This instruction of Paul shows that honoring parents Biblically is synonymous with obedience to parents. Honoring parents is definitively a cross-dispensational truth that has a place within the ins and outs of the Body of Christ.

Departing from honor and Godly parental wisdom has an effect on the life of children as they transition into young adulthood and so on.

This instruction brings an interesting point to the attention of the believer as well. Often, we hear sayings similar to "kids will be kids" or "boys will be boys." In Ephesians 6:1-3, this instruction is directed to children not parents.

This implies that children can and are expected to have a level of responsibility and understanding. But with this responsibility and understanding, like adults, parents must be graceful as they are growing in the Lord much like the children.

6:4 And, ye fathers, provoke not your children to wrath: but bring them up in the nurture and admonition of the Lord.

Now referring to fathers, we read that fathers are not to provocate children to wrath. The Bible has much to say about wrath and the Bible instructs us to forsake vengeance and wrath; because the wrath of man leads to evil (Psalm 37:8; James 1:20).

The wrath of God is just and will be carried out against those who choose to flee from the Body of Christ and His Gospel (Romans 12:19).

Godly fathers (spiritual [1 Corinthians 4:15] and physical) edify family units and build them up in the way of the Lord which is found in His word.

6:5-8 Servants, be obedient to them that are your masters according to the flesh, with fear and trembling, in singleness of your heart, as unto Christ;

Not with eyeservice, as menpleasers; but as the servants of Christ, doing the will of God from the heart;

With good will doing service, as to the Lord, and not to men:

Knowing that whatsoever good thing any man doeth, the same shall he receive of the Lord, whether he be bond or free.

As mentioned earlier, the word *servant* in its original Greek is *doulos*. This is a Greek word referring to voluntary or involuntary servitude and is often used in the same context of the word "slave".

Slavery and indentured servants were common practices in the ancient Middle East, although under much different circumstances that more modern history. Because of the commonality of the practice, Godly instruction had to be presented by Paul in how to treat each other, servants and masters.

Reading Scripture with a modern, fleshly mindset out of context will cause a confused and warped depiction of the nature of God and should be avoided.

Paul compares servanthood according to the flesh to our service to Christ. Saying this, a reverent and humble obedience is depicted. Service is contrary to selfishness.

Even in unfavorable circumstances, Paul holds servants to the high calling of Christ (Philippians 3:14), calling for Godly service and ministry for the will of God.

Our works and righteousness are as filthy rags (Isaiah 64:6) and is one reason why Jesus Christ's finished work and Gospel is so important. His righteousness is imputed upon us and we are given an inheritance which is far greater than a return on our works. Life's journey will be well worth it!

6:9 And, ye masters, do the same things unto them, forbearing threatening: knowing that your Master also is in heaven; neither is there respect of persons with him.

Masters are called to the same expectation of Godly service to their servants, knowing that they have a master in Heaven, who see them not as bondman or free, but as sons and daughters of God (Ephesians 2:19-22).

6:10-11 Finally, my brethren, be strong in the Lord, and in the power of his might.

Put on the whole armour of God, that ye may be able to stand against the wiles of the devil.

Finally, the word indicates that a conclusion is imminent; however, there is still something that must be addressed. That "something" is how to be strong in the Lord and in the power of His might.

This is the final application of practical doctrine for the letter to the Ephesians.

We must put on the whole armor of God. This is an explanation of how to be strong and powerful by the might of Jesus Christ. With our position in Christ and empowered by His armor, we can "stand against the wiles of the devil."

Paul makes it evident that we are in a war and in a fight against the Devil and his dark constructions. God makes a way to stay strong in the fight.

6:12-13 For we wrestle not against flesh and blood, but against principalities, against powers, against the rulers of the darkness of this world, against spiritual wickedness in high places.

Wherefore take unto you the whole armour of God, that ye may be able to withstand in the evil day, and having done all, to stand.

We do not wrestle against flesh and blood. We are not against people because the fact is, God desires for all men (humankind) to be saved and come unto the knowledge of the truth (1 Timothy

2:4).

Our enemy and our opposition are the dark forces contrary to God. These are listed out in verse 12. This verse is also further validation of the spiritual realm beyond that of our sight.

Yet, taking the armor of God upon us signifies a level of ownership and necessity. We *must* put on the armor of God if we want to stand firm. Not just part of the armor either, the whole armor in its entirety.

Additionally, a warrior is stronger as the Body (1 Corinthians 12:12-27) (a.k.a The Army).

This is not Paul's only allusion to being the Army of God as he also explained that the mission is to please Him who enlisted us within the Army and that we endure hardship by not entangling ourselves in the affairs of this life (2 Timothy 2:3-4).

"Having done all" means that in the end we may be found standing strong in the armor of God by His grace.

6:14-17 Stand therefore, having your loins girt about with truth, and having on the breastplate of righteousness;

And your feet shod with the preparation of the gospel of peace;

Above all, taking the shield of faith, wherewith ye shall be able to quench all the fiery darts of the wicked.

And take the helmet of salvation, and the sword of the Spirit, which is the word of God:

As Christians, we are standing in God, sealed until the day of our Redemption.

Nonetheless, staying strong in the Lord and producing fruit (Colossians 1:10; Galatians 5:22-23) is our profit. Equip the armor and produce fruit.

Once again standing, the Word instructs man to girt their loins with truth. Girting the loins is considered archaic now since the practice was a way to prepare for combat or physical activity.

It involved hiking up one's robe into a girdle or belt so that they could move swifter in combat.

Quite literally, girting out loins with truth would be comparable to the teachings of Jesus when He states, "The truth will set you free" (John 8:32). God's truth mobilizes us against spiritual opposition.

The breastplate of righteousness is the equipping and imputation of Christ's righteousness on the believer. Righteousness guards our heart in Christ Jesus and grounds us in peace (Philippians 4:7).

Spiritual opposition will try and take the Christian on in a long battle. Feet shod with peace will carry us through the long walk that the rest of Ephesians emphasizes. We are reconciled unto God into the Body of Christ and called into peace, apart from the flesh (Ephesians 2:15-17).

Therefore, we walk circumspectly, aware of the evilness that tries so hard to rid us of the peace of God (Ephesians 5:15).

When we walk in faith, we are protected from the fiery arrows of the Devil that ignite our flesh. By grace we are saved through faith (Ephesians 2:8) and have the ability to thwart the arrows that attack us relentlessly.

God is our refuge and our strength (Psalm 46:1).

Our actions and mindset should be directed by the Gospel of Jesus Christ by which we ascertain our salvation (Titus 3:5). Jesus is the head of His Body (The Church) and within our salvation, we are sealed.

We are never to take off the helmet for it is by salvation that we have the hope and assurance of victory in this spiritual war.

The Word of God is the *only* offensive weapon mentioned within the armor of God. A weapon's purpose is to damage.

The Word of God has the power to destroy the strongholds of the enemy and brings every thought into the captivity of Jesus Christ (2 Corinthians 10:3-5).

In spiritual combat, the Word of God is sharp and double-edged fulfilling many functions. It pierces soul, spirit, and heart and rescues the spiritually oppressed and is mighty to defend those who wield it (Hebrews 4:12).

In fact, we know of the armor of God, because we wield the Sword. But like any weapon, we must learn how to properly wield it.

The Bible directly tells us how to train and grow with it. Rightly dividing the Word of Truth is the Biblical approach necessary to wield the sword most efficiently (2 Timothy 2:15).

6:18-20 Praying always with all prayer and supplication in the Spirit, and watching thereunto with all perseverance and supplication for all saints;

And for me, that utterance may be given unto me, that I may open my mouth boldly, to make known the mystery of the gos-

pel,

For which I am an ambassador in bonds: that therein I may speak boldly, as I ought to speak.

Prayer, particularly supplication (a request unto God), should come with thanksgiving (Philippians 4:6) in the Spirit. Thanksgiving is often coupled with sincerity and a deep appreciation for what we are thankful for. To God, our thanksgiving can be endless.

It is the will of God that we give thanks in everything (1 Thessalonians 5:16-18).

When we pray, we are placing faith in God and for a lack of better words, energizing the armor equipped.

Therefore, pray always [18]. While we pray, remain patient and watch for the requests lifted unto the Father.

Paul urges prayer for himself as well that he may speak boldly of the Gospel. It is Scriptural to pray for and on behalf of other people. But like all prayers, God's will should be prioritized in prayer.

Paul's prayer was clearly in the will of God because it is the will of God that all men should be saved and come into the knowledge of the truth.

At the time of this writing, it is believed that Paul was, quite literally, an ambassador in bonds. If written in Rome, he would have been on trial and under house arrest.

This prayer was sincere and it was answered. The Apostle Paul preached the Gospel boldly and is one of the primary reasons we have this letter to the Ephesians.

6:21-22 But that ye also may know my affairs, and how I do, Tychicus, a beloved brother and faithful minister in the Lord, shall make known to you all things:

Whom I have sent unto you for the same purpose, that ye might know our affairs, and that he might comfort your hearts.

Tychicus, was a faithful travel companion to Paul from near Ephesus and Ephesus was his ministerial focus (Acts 20:4; 2 Timothy 4:12).

His role was similar to Paul's in to preach the Gospel, inform of Paul's condition, and comfort the hearts of the Ephesian church.

6:23-24 Peace be to the brethren, and love with faith, from God the Father and the Lord Jesus Christ.

Grace be with all them that love our Lord Jesus Christ in sincerity. Amen.

Grace and peace bookend love with faith! Grace is how God operates within this dispensation and love is the greatest attribute to flow from His graceful dispensary (1 Corinthians 13:13).

This is a great conclusion. The Lord gives grace to all that love the finisher of our faith, Jesus Christ in sincerity.

RESOURCES

Amg Pubs. (2015). Holy bible: New king james version, Hebrew-Greek Key Word Study Bible.

Blue letter bible. Blue Letter Bible. (n.d.). https://www.blueletterbible.org/.

Bullinger , E. W. (1999). *The companion Bible: The Authorized version of 1611 with the structures and Critical, explanatory, and suggestive notes and with 198 appendixes.* Kregel Publications.

Henry, M., & Church, L. F. (1961). *Commentary on the whole Bible: Genesis to Revelation.* Zondervan Pub. House.

Johnson, J. (n.d.). *Mid acts dispensational audio files.* Grace Ambassadors. https://graceambassadors.com/ephesians.

Macmillan Pub. Co. (1977). *The Macmillian Bible atlas.*

Osteen, D. (n.d.). *Study Notes from Ephesians.* Hope Bible Institute .

Trine, R. W. (2003). *This mystical life of ours: A book of suggestive thoughts for each week through the year.* Kessinger Publishing.

Vine, W. E., Kohlenberger, J. R., Swanson, J. A., & Vine, W. E. (1984). *The expanded vine's expository dictionary of new testament words.* Bethany House.

ACKNOWLEDGEMENT

I would like to make a special acknowledgement to Pastor David Osteen of Grace Bible Church. You're ministry has impacted me deeply and has inspired many of my writings of enriching-grace.com and in this commentary. I would like you to know how much of a blessing you have been as you uplift the Gospel of Jesus Christ.

ABOUT THE AUTHOR

Jacob Harris

Jacob Harris was inspired to write this commentary through his work on the ministry that he founded, Enriching Grace Ministries. Blogging fed his love of writing about the things of God and about his life. He has been a resident of a number of states including: Virginia, West Virginia, South Carolina, and currently North Carolina. At the time of this book being written, he is a senior attending Southern Wesleyan University and intends to embark on his lifelong calling as a pastor. He also proudly boasts  the hand of his loving fiance, Hallie, who constantly supports him in his various endeavors. For her, he is forever grateful.

Made in the USA
Columbia, SC
07 October 2022

69018427R00041